Library of Contemporary Architects

EERO SAARINEN

Library of Contemporary Architects

EERO SAARINEN

Introduction and notes by
RUPERT SPADE

with 70 photographs by
YUKIO FUTAGAWA

SIMON AND SCHUSTER NEW YORK

Copyright © 1971 by Thames and Hudson Ltd, London
Photographs copyright © 1968 by Yukio Futagawa

Published in the United States by Simon and Schuster
Rockefeller Center, 630 Fifth Avenue
New York, New York 10020

First U.S. printing

First published in Japan in 1968 by Bijutsu Shuppan-sha, Tokyo, in their series
GENDAI KENCHIKUKA SHIRIZU.
New texts have been provided for this English language edition.

SBN 671-20879-9
Library of Congress Catalog Card Number: 70-139584

Printed in Japan

Contents

Introduction   7

The Plates   21

Notes on the plates   117

Chronological list: projects and events   125

Select bibliography   127

Index   129

Introduction

'If the structural developments which have led to our present technical skill were to continue at the same pace into this century, at a pace that is, exceeding our capacity as artists to assimilate them, then our hopes of establishing a workable architecture would be slight.'

E. Maxwell Fry (1944)

Eero Saarinen was born in 1910, forty-one years after Frank Lloyd Wright, twenty-four years after Mies van der Rohe, twenty-three years after Le Corbusier, and twenty-seven years after Walter Gropius. His death at the age of fifty-one occurred only two years after that of Wright, and before those of the other giants of the modern movement. Thus Saarinen, while not of the heroic generation by birth, was by death: a paradox which has confused successive critical assessments. He tends either to be classed with the epic heroes—despite the fact that he built nothing truly his own[1] until after the death of his father Eliel Saarinen in 1950—or to be unfavourably contrasted with them as an architect of the second rank. Both views are in error. Saarinen junior neither struggled against a hostile world (in the manner of the young Corbusier), nor was he an inferior creative talent. Instead he took over the solid commercial success of his father's American practice and in ten years of unremitting work tried to do something with it that no other commercially successful architect had ever succeeded in doing—he tried to overtake the fast-moving train of technology (of which the English architect Maxwell Fry wrote so perceptively in the passage quoted above), and impose upon it a system of checks and balances similar in effect to the discipline of classical and Renaissance architecture. The task, by the fifth decade of the twentieth century, was already beyond the scope of any one man—probably beyond the scope of any human institution—and in the event cancer ended his tremendous effort almost before it had begun. As a consequence Eero Saarinen's buildings lie sprinkled about the United States and Europe like discarded fragments of some great design which never finally took shape at all. To search for a stylistic continuity or a consistent theory of design within these buildings is futile: the consistency lay in Saarinen's head, in the desperate pursuit of an ideal from which not even life itself could distract him in the end.

9

'Hvitträsk', the house where Eero Saarinen was born, stands overlooking a lake eighteen miles from Helsinki. It was built by his father in 1902, in a Finland which was still a Grand Duchy in the Imperial Russian confederation—itself so soon to give place to Lenin's Soviet Union. The population of the country at that time was just under three million, of whom about ninety per cent. were Finns and the remainder of Swedish descent; to this day there are two official languages in Finland in recognition of this ethnic division, and the influence of Sweden, which ruled Finland between 1323 and 1809, is still culturally paramount.

The house itself was a rambling, 38-roomed mansion built as combined studio and living space by three graduates of the Helsinki Polytechnic Institute, of whom the best known was Eliel Saarinen. The three had won a competition in 1899 for the design of the Finnish pavilion at the Paris exhibition of 1900—a success which enabled them to set up in practice. After the partnership's success in the 1904 competition for Helsinki Central railway station, Saarinen senior increasingly took over the whole of 'Hvitträsk'; one by one his partners left, and between 1907 and 1923, when he left for the United States, he lived and worked there with only his own family.

The design for the railway station—or more particularly the process by which it was designed—revealed something of the obsessive energy and determination which Saarinen junior was later to bring to the same task. Eliel Saarinen took his family on a lengthy tour of major railway termini throughout Europe, he studied the mechanics of railway operation and discussed the problems of railway design with numerous experts; in view of his son's later researches in airport design this process shows an acute similarity in work method. Completed in 1914, the building marks the end of the romantic national phase in favour of the rationalism which was later to make Finnish design famous.

The close of the First World War saw Finland drawn for the first time into the burgeoning conflict between Germany and Russia. A brief but bloody civil war succeeded the granting of Finnish independence by Lenin in 1917, and the Finnish Bolsheviks were put to flight by right-wing forces led by Marshal Mannerheim. In June 1919 Finland was declared a republic, to be admitted to the League of Nations a year later.

The early 1920s were difficult years for European architects in general and nowhere more so than in Finland where inflation had carried the exchange rate of the Finnish mark against sterling from 25 in 1914 to 244 in 1922. Major commissions were few and far between and the demands of national reconstruction allied to the necessity for an increasing exploitation of the country's natural resources placed architecture low on the list of national priorities. To this Eliel Saarinen had little to contribute, he was an architect in the nineteenth-century mould, and a 20,000 dollar second prize in the *Chicago Tribune* competition of 1922 lured him to the United States—he was then forty-nine.

After a short time in New York the Saarinen family moved on into the Middle West and by 1925 were established at Cranbrook, north of Detroit. Here, under the patronage of auto-millionaire George C. Booth, Eliel constructed a school which was in spirit a second 'Hvitträsk'. Here the intellectual discourse and creative work of the pre-1914 period reconvened for a further twenty-five years, during which time Eero (thirteen years old at the time of the emigration) grew up as an *émigré* Finn—returning to his homeland every summer until 1939.

Cranbrook, like Frank Lloyd Wright's Taliesin East, constituted an oasis of modern architectural thought in what Daniel Burnham called 'one vast desert of the bozar'. Wright himself had a low opinion of Saarinen senior, characterizing him patronizingly as 'the best of the eclectics', and there was no contact between the two schools—except insofar as they formed stopping places for modern enthusiasts passing from west to east or vice versa. Nonetheless, when Eero abandoned his earlier ambition to become a sculptor—which had taken him to La Grande Chaumière in Paris—he repaired not to the Bauhaus, Taliesin, or Cranbrook, but to Yale, where an orthodox 'bozar' course loaded him with honours on graduation in 1934. The capacity to work well within an apparently limiting framework, which he demonstrated during his three years at Yale, was to remain a valuable attribute throughout his life. Like Mies van der Rohe he always contrived to convey a kind of respect for position, authority and money which enabled him to combine unorthodox, even heretical design thinking with the allegiance of conservative, institutional clients of enormous wealth.

Following his graduation Eero did not immediately return to Cranbrook but worked for a time with Norman Bel Geddes, a connection which led to a meeting with Charles Eames in 1937. Pursuing their joint interest in advanced furniture design—Eero had designed the furniture for a large school project of his father's in 1929—he invited Eames to take over the Department of Experimental Design at Cranbrook. Eames accepted and joined Florence Knoll, Harry Weese, Ralph Rapson, Harry Bertoia and others later to achieve distinction in their own fields, on the teaching staff of the establishment. Eames and Eero collaborated over the design of a range of furniture using rubber-bonded plywood and metal for an organic design competition sponsored by the New York Museum of Modern Art in 1940. They won first prize in each of the two main categories but America's entry into the Second World War in 1941 caused the exhibition of competition entries to be postponed until 1946 when, fortuitously, plywood bonding and construction techniques had advanced sufficiently for the range to be an economic manufacturing proposition. Although Eames left Cranbrook after his marriage in 1941 the contact between the two men remained unbroken until Eero's death; Eames collaborated over the brief for the architect's most famous commission, Dulles International Airport, Washington, D.C., completed posthumously in 1962.

The coming of the Second World War in Europe effectively ended the dual nationality of the Saarinen family and involvement in Defense Department housing at Willow Run and Center Line, Michigan, committed both father and son to a level of architectural practice without parallel in the experience of either. One of Eero's earliest attempts to stretch the building technology of his time began with the design of a prototype 'unfolding house', whose flexible aluminium roof could be unrolled to accommodate additional rooms—a project which originated under the aegis of the National Housing Association.

With the conclusion of the war the Saarinen office found itself in possession of several very important commissions, probably the most challenging of which was the enormous 20 million dollar General Motors Technical Center outside Detroit. When this project had first been mooted General Motors approached Eliel Saarinen with a view to building a technical centre rather like Cranbrook itself. Preliminary designs had been prepared but the project lapsed for three years, only to resume with increased force on the crest of a wave of post-war automobile sales. In 1948 a centre was proposed whose scale far exceeded the magnitude of the original Cranbrook model—this time General Motors envisaged the development of a 900-acre flat site at Warren, Michigan, and the expenditure of around 100 million dollars. It was at this point that, by common consent, the commission devolved from the seventy-five year old father to the thirty-eight year old son: Eero thus took control of the largest and most opulent commission ever awarded to a modern architect up to that time. The original sketches of 1945 were still however to have their effect. Eliel's compact, expressionistic grouping of buildings around an immense lake formed the nucleus of Eero's much expanded concept, although the aerofoil-shaped Research Building—reminiscent of the streamform images of the 1930s—was to disappear under the impact of the son's more classic interpretation of the formal needs of the Technical Center.

The conception of an appropriate form and structure underlay both Eero's ability to inspire the hard-headed businessmen of General Motors, and his extraordinary determination, in his own words, 'to base the design on steel—the metal of the automobile . . . and base the construction on the advanced technology of the automobile age.'[2] His initial stretching of Eliel's densely integrated group of buildings sprang from a conviction that just as automobile speed vastly exceeded walking speed, so should automobile distances vastly exceed walking distances. As a consequence the plan was re-articulated with all its basic elements clearly separated and the whole composition arranged around a ten-storey office building springing from the 22-acre lake. This 1949 version is generally felt by critics to have been the best[3] but a revised brief speedily put an end to the office building, and its replacement by a 132-ft tripod water tower and 50×100 ft 'water wall' (pumping more water than all the fountains at Versailles)[4] tended to stress even more the vast, echoing emptiness of the whole composition. Saarinen's image of a perspective vista foreshortened by a high-speed automobile approach has not on the whole been admired. Like HALT signs painted on the surface of a road the arrangement of the separate departments at General Motors requires the static foreshortening effect of the camera to create the illusion of compactness evident in photographs of the complex: a visit to the airport-sized site tends to be differently received:

'The emptiness of the long, open side of the lake is reminiscent of a de Chirico anxiety painting: the individual finds himself in an unpeopled abstraction of industrial civilization, strangely cowed by distant forms.'[5]

The abandonment of the basic qualities of the 1945 and 1949 concepts was confirmed after Eliel Saarinen's death in 1950. In the buildings themselves (though not over the entire site, as in the case of the Illinois Institute of Technology campus by Mies van der Rohe, with which General Motors is often compared), Eliel adopted a small five-foot module for the steel and glass curtain-walling system which—in conjunction with the research and development department of General Motors—his office devised to meet his own dictum that the design should use the technology of the automobile age. His own description of this achievement gives some indication of the extent to which he already felt destined to revolutionize the building industry as a whole.

'General Motors represents the first significant installation of laminated panels and the first use anywhere of a uniquely thin porcelain-faced sandwich panel which is a complete prefabricated wall for both exterior and interior ... The ceilings in the drafting rooms are the first developed completely luminous ceilings using special modular plastic pans. Perhaps the greatest gift to the building industry is the development [or rather adaptation from auto-windshield use] of the neoprene gasket weather seal, which holds fixed glass and porcelain enamel metal panels to their aluminium frames. It is truly windproof and waterproof and is capable of allowing the glass or panels to be "zipped out" whenever a building's use changes. All of these developments have since become part of the building industry ...'[6]

Thus having conceived a complex of buildings 'essentially put together, as on an assembly line, out of mass-produced units',[7] Eero felt sure that he had established a basic building technology for the automobile industry and of the automobile industry. Carping criticism could be stilled by the grandeur and astronomical cost of it all; besides there were other areas of building technology to upgrade—other generic building types to revolutionize. Throughout the construction period of the General Motors Technical Center, Saarinen's office continued to expand. Further enormous projects came into his enthusiastic and tireless hands, the staff rose from ten to fifty, and finally to ninety. Day and night, even on Christmas Eve,[8] Saarinen worked. The race was on.

The next realization, following an abortive design study for a new north campus at the University of Michigan, was the Kresge Auditorium and Chapel at the Massachusetts Institute of Technology, completed in 1956. This pair of buildings (which the architect even as little as five years later had referred to as his 'early work') clearly demonstrated the nature of Saarinen's design process and the meaning of the slogan 'methodical but not cautious'[9] which he endorsed in relation to himself. Both structures were geometrically based: the auditorium a thin concrete shell derived from one-eighth part of a sphere; the chapel a cylinder in brick with a blind-arched base and a superimposed tripod belfry and spire. The handsome Yale University Press edition of Saarinen's collected works included a page of sketches for the latter with remarks to the effect that the architect intended to spend the weekend working with 'plastocene' (sic) on the design of the belfry, producing numerous rough models for his own model-maker to realize later 'in more permanent form'.

The auditorium itself, despite its bold sectional conception, turned out in the end to possess not a little of the awkwardness associated with combining a dominant, curvilinear form with uncompromisingly vertical glazing. Here again Saarinen constructed 'dozens of models', but the result still had the look and feel of a hastily worked-up sketch design. Temporary disorganization may account for this. During the period of design work the architect's thirteen-year marriage to former Cranbrook ceramics student Lily Swann broke up; following the death of his father and the sudden expansion of his office this led to a temporary hiatus during which, as Temko notes, 'new men, brilliant as some of them were, did not immediately understand—as some of their predecessors had—what Eero meant by a nod or a grunt. Inevitably, Saarinen briefly lost full control.'[10]

There are photographs of the architect during this period, working late at night over large-sized models. He smokes continually, his shirt collar is loose and his sleeves rolled up. Around him stand assistants in the uncomfortable postures of those anxious to be given jobs to do and the privacy to get on with them undisturbed. Saarinen is a man obsessed: without a country, without a father, without a wife, he works.

High in the sky over Minnesota in the depths of the winter of 1955/56 flies a light plane; its windows are frozen over to the point of opacity, the two passengers peer over the pilot's shoulders trying to see the ground through the windshield—the only electrically heated window in the plane: Eero Saarinen and Kevin Roche (chief of his design staff) are on a site visit. Far below them lies a snow-covered patch of ground on which will soon stand the first of the architect's major commissions from International Business Machines (IBM): the Electronics and Administration Buildings at Rochester. Saarinen smokes his pipe and thinks. Eventually the plane lands. 'Architecture', he obscurely remarks, 'consists of placing something between earth and sky.'[11]

At IBM the requirement was for growth, in large modules of 60,000 sq. ft of manufacturing, and 40,000 sq. ft of administration space. Order was necessary so that this growth should not destroy the identity of what had gone before. Beyond that was a need for the building to express the new character of the technological revolution: light electronic engineering at Rochester would not produce smoke, effluent or noise. The invisible function of the plant would not of itself generate simplistic formal interpretations such as those which had so inspired Erich Mendelsohn in the early decades of the century. Something more sophisticated, more relaxed, was needed. Once again Saarinen turned to the curtain wall, the thin membrane separating environmentally controlled space from the elements; on each of the bland, rectangular blocks which constituted the IBM 'campus' he imprinted the frozen, reflecting blue of a wrap-around glass façade.

'For its time this was the thinnest enclosure of such insulating value (equal to a 16 inch brick wall) ever developed. The spandrels of sandwich construction here have become 'wafers' only $\frac{5}{16}$ of an inch thick (compared with $2\frac{1}{2}$ inches at General Motors). They are simply fine layers of aluminium porcelainised on the exterior, which have been laminated to an asbestos core. The neoprene gasket has become a more efficient weather seal than at G.M., and virtually every other respect these surfaces are among the most economical ever devised.'[12]

The concept of an isolated, out of town, prestige 'research' or 'development' centre, operating and looking like a very exclusive school, appealed to IBM and other large American corporations. Clad in the impenetrable armour of the International Style, built of the highest quality materials, yet light, shiny and *mechanical* somehow, the very image of General Motors and Rochester begat further commissions. In 1956 Saarinen received approaches from both IBM and the Bell Telephone Corporation on the subject of similar research centres set in parkland sites. As before the budgets were to be enormous, the technical requirements exacting and the prestige value of the resultant buildings not to be minimized: in 1957 the architect began work on both projects simultaneously.

For him the concept of the prestige research centre held many similarities to that of the country house of previous centuries. Like many predecessors, he carefully landscaped large areas, led access roads through groves of trees to provide fleeting glimpses of the building itself, provided imposing views and ensured privacy by acres of tree-planting. On the IBM site at Yorktown he placed a crescent-shaped, curtain-walled building around the top of a small hill. The façade was over 1,000 feet long and the approach to it led past a lake created by the architect. Eventually, he announced, the growth of IBM would lead to a complete circling of the hill-crest and the fortress of technology would be complete. The planning of the centre itself reflected by the analytical care which Saarinen could put into the *organization* of a building, a care which was also a characteristic of his father's work. Here a study of similar research facilities throughout the country led him to conclude that the conventional use of internal corridors (to permit the daylighting of laboratories) was unrelated to the facts of modern scientific life. At the Murray Hill Facility of Bell Telephone Corporation he noticed that blinds in the perimeter laboratories were nearly always closed and daylighting hardly ever employed, whilst the internal corridors tended to be noisy and claustrophobic spaces. At Yorktown he reversed his current orthodoxy by running corridors against the glazed outer walls back and front of the laboratories, themselves top-lit only. The glazed walls themselves were yet further refinements on the General Motors pattern at Rochester.

'Saarinen was able to dispense with the horizontal spandrel (since the curtain walls enclosed only corridors) by running the near-black glass from floor to ceiling. Only fine metal strips separate the triple bank of tall panes at the floor levels, so that the effect is of a continuous glass surface from the base of the building to the roof.'[13]

The contemporary Bell Laboratories complex at Holmdel, New Jersey, exhibited an even more grandiloquent indulgence in the landscape world of Louis XIV. Providing over one million square feet of office space and housing 4,000 scientific workers, the huge rectangular building was placed across the centre of an immense ellipse itself broken by two smaller ellipses with the building placed centrally between them. The scale of landscaping, tree-planting and formalized approach exceeds both Rochester and Yorktown, whilst the building itself, curtain-walled in mirror glass for the purpose of reducing air-conditioning load, is planned on two axes with complete symmetry.

Saarinen's last glass and steel commission in the Royal Hunting Lodge *genre* was the headquarters of Deere & Company, completed at Moline, Illinois, in 1963 after his death. Here once again was a 600-acre site, this time as undulating and wooded as the Holmdel site had been bare and flat. Saarinen once again created a lake, as at Rochester, but this time he ran it from beneath a bridging administration building, where it is formally laid out as a rectangle, down via a stream to a lower level where it spreads out into a roughly circular form beneath overhanging trees. On either side of the seven-storey administration building flying bridges lead to the laboratory block and the exhibition hall, both of which have fewer storeys but, being set further up the slope of the valley, reach the same height as the central block. The winding access road approaches the complex from the floor of the valley.

In considering an appropriate form of construction for the head-quarters of a company manufacturing agricultural machinery. Saarinen reflected on the necessity for a 'bold and direct . . . strong and basic building . . . not slick, precise, glittering glass and spindly metal.'[14] He hit upon the answer in the use of a high-tensile steel alloy whose process of oxidation was effectively self-arresting after the development of a cinnamon-brown coloured patina over the exposed surface. This steel, frequently used in engineering work, was a hitherto unused medium for architectural expression, and was of course rather more expensive than conventional mild steel. Eager to test the aesthetic possibilities of the material, Saarinen authorized the construction of a full-size mock up of one end elevation of the laboratory block, allowing it to rust under scrutiny for one year. So successful was the experiment that the design was modified to expose more and more steel in the form of *brise soleil*, balconies with checkerplate floor panels, and exposed roof members. The original glass screen walls—using mirror glass again, this time tinted gold—recede behind this steel tracery, making the whole building resemble a scaffolding framework rather than a solid form.

Altogether different was the last of his major corporation commissions, the Columbia Broadcasting System (CBS) headquarters in New York City. Here, a little later than Mies van der Rohe's bronze-clad Seagram Building, came Eero's contribution to the Manhattan skyline —a massive granite-clad, concrete-framed building zooming thirty-eight storeys into the sky without a break in its profile. Intended originally to stand like its Seagram counterpart in a large 'public space', the building was for financial reasons finally confined to a sunken piazza little larger than the area of the base itself. As a result it retains little of the grandeur of the Seagram Building. Restrictions on the ground-floor treatment resulted from CBS's insistence on provision for commercial premises there, an effect aggravated by Saarinen's own inexplicable miniaturization of the side entrances (set between triangular columns at close centres), and his refusal to provide any entrance at all on the narrow side facing the main thoroughfare. In an imperious gesture the architect decreed complete control over the interior of the building: offices are furnished and equipped according to a rigid schedule and, apart from the President of CBS himself, no one is allowed to modify it. A former Cranbrook teacher, Florence Knoll, was appointed interior designer for the block.

Magnificent as were Saarinen's achievements as *château* builder to the new American institutional aristocracy, they were dwarfed in scale and promise by his ventures in airport design—just as in national renown they were minimized by his twin competition-winning designs for the United States embassies in London and Oslo. Both the embassies, the TWA terminal at Idlewild (now Kennedy) Airport, New York, and the

16

Dulles International Airport buildings, Washington, D.C., were executed in concrete—a material with which the architect had experimented before, notably on the Milwaukee War Memorial and the Ingalls Hockey Rink at Yale. The last two buildings were both boldly conceived structural *tours de force* making considerable demands on the abilities of the structural engineers employed to make them stand up. Unfortunately the dedicated work of these men—Ammann and Whitney for the memorial and Fred Severud for the rink—was not matched by the architect's own attention to detail. During the final design phase of the Milwaukee memorial Eero was heavily occupied with the London embassy, and during the speedy completion of the rink he was already totally immersed in the design of the great 'frozen bird' at Idlewild. The results were consequently somewhat less exciting than at first promised, the bold initial conceptions being marred by garish finishes and in appropriate details.

Much the same can be (and has been) said of his embassy designs. Working at top speed with a staff nine times greater than that employed by the office at the time of his father's death, Eero contrived increasingly to confuse intention with achievement. Writing of the London embassy he noted[15] that the choice of Portland stone would in time, with 'London soot and rain and wind . . . make a dramatically dark building.' Similarly he hoped that the choice of materials would 'create a stateliness and formality'.[16] In practice the building was almost unanimously condemned by British critics, the square in which it stood was obliterated by the architect's failure to use all the site (thus opening the corners in a most unhappy way), the anticipated soot failed to materialize (as a result of the Clean Air Act of 1956), and the gold anodised-aluminium trimmings to the façade created an effect at once cheap and garish. Even the giant eagle atop the centre (which Saarinen wanted to be even larger) failed to ignite the enthusiasm of Americanophiles. Characteristically—as we might think—he replied to such criticisms with an ingenious backhander: 'the building is much better than the English think—but not quite as good as I wished it to be.'[17]

By 1956, when the TWA terminal commission arrived, Eero had remarried—this time to an art critic named Aline Louchheim whose life style was more compatible with his own frenetic travelling and working. Her admiration for his work began before their marriage and was the subject of an almost embarrassing encomium entitled 'Now Saarinen the Son' published in the *New York Times* in 1953. In this article she claimed that Eero was chiefly concerned with 'giving form or visual order to the industrial civilization to which he belongs', and it is in this sense that his now famous airport commissions should be interpreted. Of TWA Temko notes:

'The building was conceived as an emotional instrument resounding with monumental harmonies. The traveller would feel the unfolding power of its symphonic motive as soon as he passed through the aspiring front supports . . . upward on convergent stairs into the crescendo of the central space. . . Through the enormous convex windows, slanting upward and outward, there would be elating views of runways and the sky: and glazed bridgeways—springing from the main building to the heraldic departure stations—equipped with moving sidewalks to complete the kinetic effect.'[18]

In keeping with this ecstatic conception was the reaction of the architectural world at the time of the publication of the first design studies during the late 1950s. Probably no other project of the period—with the exception of Utzon's ill-fated Sydney Opera House—generated such wild acclaim. For a time, in the minds of those who had observed his meteoric career, Saarinen really seemed to have caught up with satellites, jetliners, gas-turbine cars and the whole technological *zeitgeist*. Unhappily the triumph was—in part at least—illusory. The chaotic architectural environment of Idlewild, where every major airline had its own building, drowned the soaring shape of the great bird—never quite as big as it appeared in photographs. Worse still, unresolved movement problems dogged the whole operational premise on which the building had been conceived, the moving pavements were discarded and the bridgeways completed as simple tunnels. Even the construction of the concrete shells themselves (engineers: Ammann and Whitney) subtly but remorselessly eroded the kinetic energy implicit in the original conception. Minute increments of change made the building heavier, absurd steel balustrading with closely packed rails destroyed the integrity of the interior, glazing bars broke up the flow of space from one volume to the next. 'It would make a beautiful ruin, like the baths of Caracalla,' observed the architect[19] shortly before his death—at which time only the concrete vaults had been completed.

One further airport commission lay within his grasp. This time, a bare three years before the end, he was entrusted with the design of an entire airport system—the first in the world intended exclusively for jets. He resolved that the congestion of Idlewild as much as the impossible distances at Chicago's O'Hare Airport would be avoided. The 'finger' pattern of terminal design had outlived its usefulness; with the steady increase in the size of aircraft the distances to be walked by passengers had reached intolerable levels. As a man habituated to the miseries of air travel Saarinen resolved to invent something new for the Dulles International Airport, Washington, D.C.

He embarked on the problem with characteristic energy. Teams were sent out with counters and stop watches to see what people really do at airports; technical reports and air force experience of jet operation were analysed; loading schedules, turn-round times, peak loads, the effects of weather, baggage handling, crowd control and movement systems studied and compared. At length the solution arrived in the form of an adaptation of the 'primitive' system of shuttle-bus carriage still used to transport passengers at many European airports.

'The soundest system seemed to be one which brought the passenger to the plane rather than the plane to the passenger. . . Gradually, we arrived at the concept of a mobile lounge; a departure lounge on stilts and wheels, a part of the terminal which detaches itself from the building and travels out to wherever the plane is conveniently parked or serviced.'[20]

Thus the mobile departure lounges were conceived, enormous vehicles capable of carrying plane loads of passengers from the centralized airport building—itself a *tour de force* in prestressed and precast concrete—to waiting planes at various points on the airfield. An answer which in a sense transcended the limitations of architecture altogether

18

by espousing *movement*, the guiding principle of the technology Saarinen had for so long pursued. In this massive, terminal work (which he himself considered to be his masterpiece),[21] he was finally able to integrate his concept of architecture with the developing technology of the twentieth century. The mobile departure lounges succeeded where the stillborn moving pavements of the TWA building had failed in that the long tentacles of Saarinen's architecture reached beyond the static confines of the central building into that elastic space between points which has become in our era the arena for the most spectacular and penetrating miracles of technology. The beginnings of a massive, flexible welding together of static and mobile elements into an architecture of the future started at Dulles airport. And just before his death Saarinen seemed to be beginning that sacrifice of static, monumental form which may well become the talisman of the architecture of the twenty-first century.

Twelve years before the design of his masterpiece, and before the death of his father, Eero Saarinen won a competition for the design of the Jefferson Westward Expansion Memorial at St Louis, Missouri. For ten years he waited for a railway to be relocated and then, in 1958, work began. A huge arch, clad in stainless steel, containing small lift cars to transport sightseers to the 630-ft high observation room, now stands on the banks of the Mississippi river. Here in a way Saarinen's quest both began and ended: the first major design to separate him from the work of his father (both had entered the competition separately), and one of the last to be completed after his own death, the Jefferson Memorial expresses both the ambition and the emptiness of the architect's meteoric career. It is after all a simple arch, a form known to the ancients and associated with architecture for some thousands of years; but it is also a hollow-frame structure, engineered with considerable skill and daring. More like a circulatory system than a skeleton, it is crammed with unseen movement. Seen from a distance the simple form is deceptive, inside is the seething technology of a new world, waiting to get out.

1 'Until his death in 1950, when I started to create my own form, I worked within the form of my father.' *Eero Saarinen on his Work*, ed. Aline B. Saarinen, New Haven, Conn., and London, 1962

2 Ibid.

3 Sherban Cantacuzino (*Great Modern Architecture*, New York and London, 1966), and Allan Temko (*Eero Saarinen*, London and New York, 1962), agree about this, as does Peter Carter ('Eero Saarinen, 1910–1961', in *Architectural Design*, December 1961)

4 Sherban Cantacuzino, *Great Modern Architecture*

5 Allan Temko, *Eero Saarinen*

6 *Eero Saarinen on his Work*

7 Ibid.

8 Allan Temko, *Eero Saarinen*

9 *Eero Saarinen on his Work*

10 Allan Temko, *Eero Saarinen*

11 Ibid.

12 Ibid.

13 Ibid.

14 *Eero Saarinen on his Work*

15 *Ibid.*

16 Ibid.

17 Ibid.

18 Allan Temko, *Eero Saarinen*

19 *Eero Saarinen on his Work*

20 Ibid.

21 Ibid.: on 21 June 1961, two months before his death, Saarinen remarked, 'I think this airport is the best thing I have done. I think it is going to be really good. Maybe it will even explain what I believe about architecture.'

The Plates

**1-5, Jefferson Memorial Arch, St Louis, Missouri
(competition 1947-48; built 1959-64)**

1 The triangular base, with 50-ft sides, of one leg of the arch

2 The arch in relation to the nearby East river bridge

3 The full span of the arch

1

4

4, 5 Views from below, showing
the tiny observation windows at the
vertex, and stainless-steel cladding

6-10, General Motors Technical Center, Warren, Michigan (1948-56)

6 The main gate leading to the Technical Center

7 Plan of the Technical Center, showing arrangement of buildings around the central lake, access roads and extensive perimeter tree-planting

6

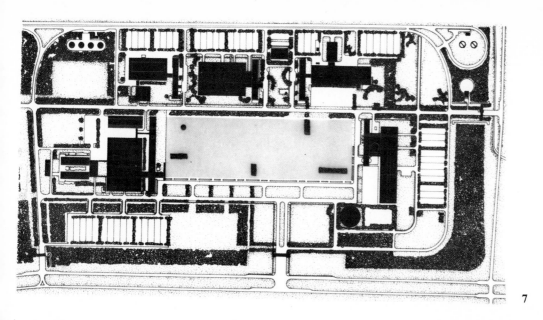

7

8 An administrative block, with external sculpture set against the precision of the curtain-walled exterior

9 The styling dome, a steel-clad hemisphere whose reflections in the sun tend to destroy the outline when seen from a distance

10 The 120-ft tripod water tower clad in stainless steel and springing from the floor of the lake

8

9

**11-15, The Kresge Chapel,
Massachusetts Institute
of Technology,
Cambridge, Mass. (1953-56)**

11   The covered way linking the
narthex and the chapel

12   Plan of chapel and narthex,
showing: 1, main entrance; 2,
circular chapel; 3, narthex with
auxiliary accommodation

13 External view of the chapel
showing superimposed tripod belfry
and blind and open arches at base

14 Top-lighting on to the white
marble altar via Harry Bertoia's
suspended golden screen

15 The arch abutments at the foot
of the rough-brick chapel drum
contrast with the smooth finish of
the neighbouring Kresge auditorium

16, 17
The Kresge Auditorium,
Massachusetts Institute
of Technology,
Cambridge, Mass. (1953-56)

16 Internal view of the auditorium
showing curvature of seating and
shell as well as suspended acoustic
baffles

17 Sectional view through auditorium

16

17

18-22, The Law School, University of Chicago, Chicago, Illinois (1956-60)

18 (*overleaf*) The main façade of the Law School showing ventilation outlets at the top of each triangular section of curtain wall

19 Small auditoria at the rear, sometimes used as courtrooms

20 Plans of three floors of the Law School: 1, foyer and lounge at ground-floor level; 2, first-floor reading rooms; 3, library; 4, studies

21 Ground-floor foyer

22 Library annex

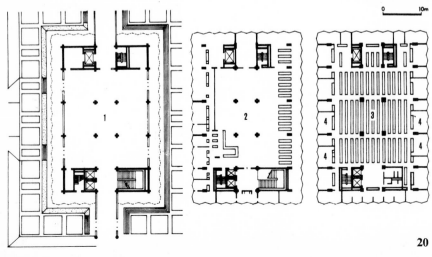

0   10m

23-25, U.S. Chancellery building, London, England (1955-60)

23 The U.S. Chancellery seen from Grosvenor Square. Saarinen wished the huge eagle to be larger still

24 Plan of principal floor of the Chancellery, showing: 1, foyer; 2, side entrance; 3, entrance to United States Information Service; 4, library

25 Interior and exhibition space

23

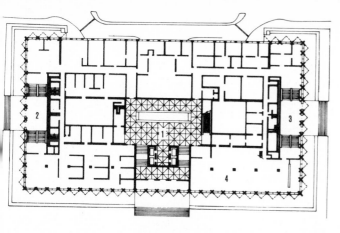

24

26-31, U.S. Chancellery building, Oslo, Norway (1955-59)

26

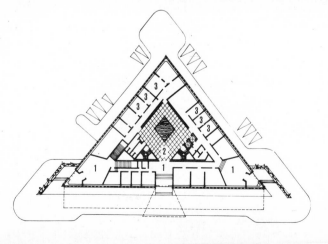

27

26 Corner of principal façade

27 Plan of principal floor of the Chancellery: 1, entrance foyers; 2, central court; 3, administrative offices

28 Articulated treatment of granite-faced precast façades

29 The cantilevered entrance canopy with flagstaff

30

30 Glazed roof of the central court

31 The central court with pool and seating

32-35, International Business Machines: Thomas A. Watson
Research Center, Yorktown, N.Y. (1957-61)

32

32 The Japanese garden by
Sasaki, Walker & Associates at the
rear of the research centre

33 Site plan of the research centre,
showing winding approach road,
artificial lake, and direction chosen
for the expansion of the part-
circular building

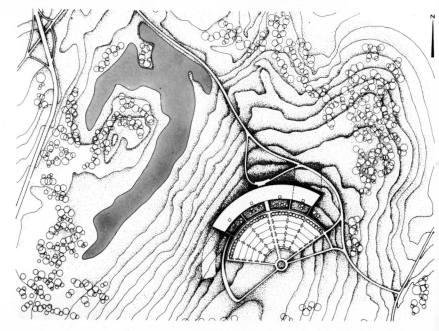

34 A sculpture by Seymour Lipton
atop its rubble wall in front of
the curtain-walled façade

35 The curved façade of the
research centre, showing uniform
glazing and cantilevered entrance
canopy

36-40, Bell Telephone Corporation Research Laboratories, Holmdel, New Jersey (1957-62)

36 The exterior mirror-glazed curtain wall seen from one of the lateral access bridges

37 Site plan showing extensive baroque landscaping of the large site

38 The main façade of the 700-ft block

39 Ground-floor plan of the building, showing: 1, utility areas; 2, laboratories

40 Main façade of the block showing entrance canopy and opaque mirror glass

36

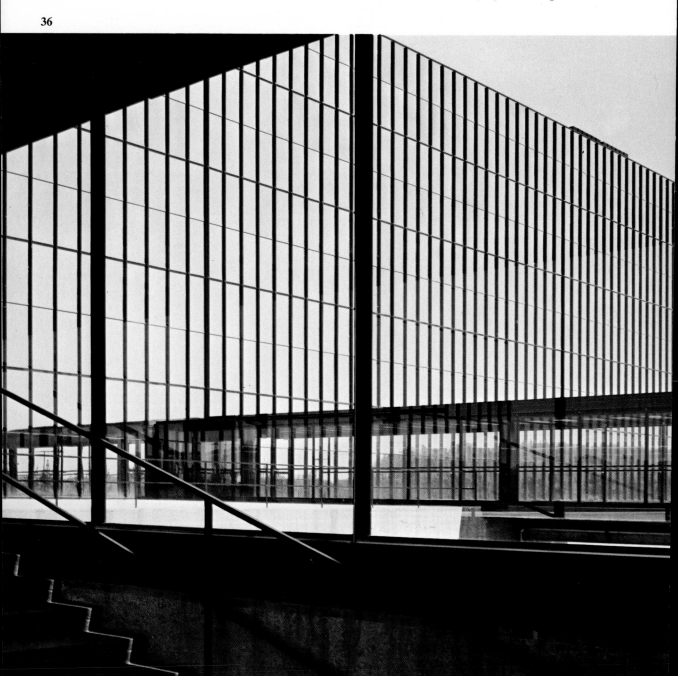

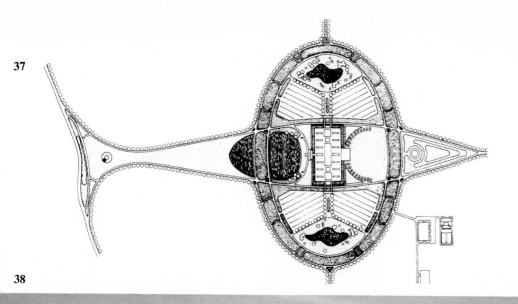

37

38

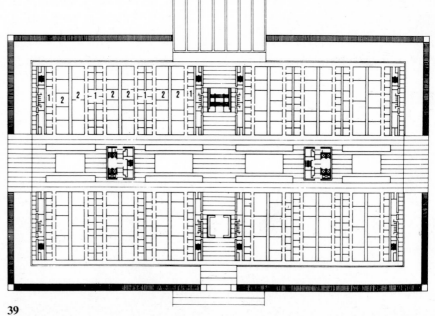

39

**41-43, Irwin Union Bank and Trust Company,
Columbus, Indiana (1952-55)**

41

42

43

41 Low-level external lighting
standard

42 The single-storey banking hall,
showing recessed reflectors

43 Entrance to the banking hall
and fair-faced brick side wall to
office building

**44-47, Milwaukee County War Memorial, Milwaukee,
Wisconsin (1953-57)**

44-46 Section and floor plans of
War Memorial, showing cantilevers
and internal circulation: 1, central
open court; 2, veterans' meeting
room; 3, offices

47 The memorial on its hill-top
site, showing two of the three
cantilevered blocks with their
polyhedral support columns

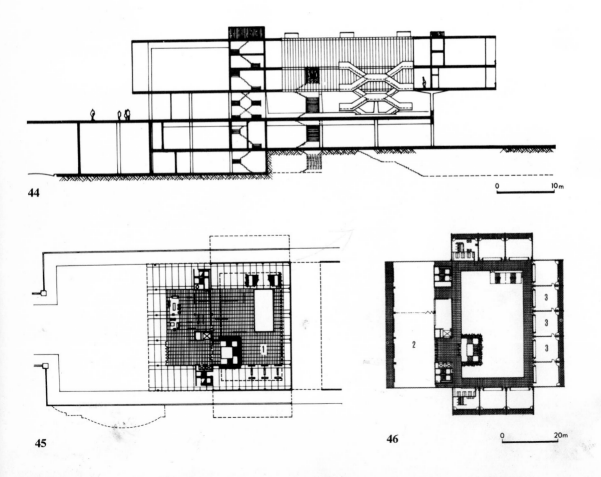

44

0   10 m

45

46

0   20m

48-52, David S. Ingalls Hockey Rink, Yale University, New Haven, Connecticut (1956-59)

48 Interior of the rink. Catenary cables and close boarding can be seen, as can the full sweep of the parabolic support arch

49, 50 Plan and section of the rink, showing: 1, main entrance; 2, exhibition space; 3, access ramps to seating; 4, exit stairs to car parking areas; 5, press box; 6, players' boxes

51 Side view of the Ingalls rink showing sloping side walls

52 The main entrance to the rink showing sculptured floodlighting mounted on the end of the cantilevered extension to the main arch beam. Two of the three auxiliary support cables can also be seen

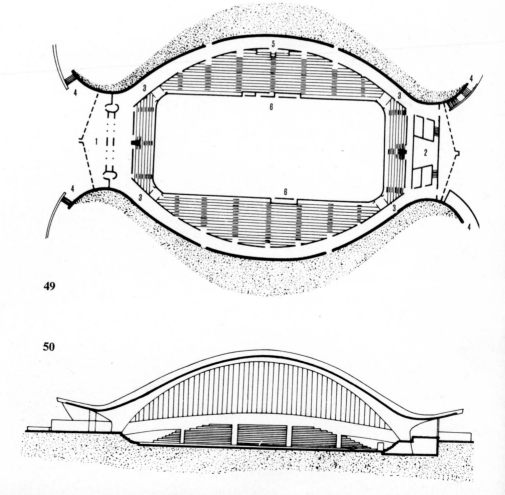

49

50

51

53-60, Trans World Airlines terminal building, Idlewild (now Kennedy) Airport, New York, N.Y. (1956-62)

53

53 The entrance to the terminal from the parking area

54 Sectional drawing of TWA terminal, showing general arrangement beneath the four major vaults

55 One of the huge Y-shaped columns supporting the four major vaults

56 The central staircase area beneath the intersection of the four vaults. Despite bold efforts Saarinen's 'family of forms' is not entirely consistent: glazing and balustrading defeat the curvilinear shapes within

57 Japanese mosaic tiles cover the cantilevered desk and departure board in the ticket lobby

58 One of the curvilinear service wings which reach out from beneath the concrete vaults

59 A sunken lounge space overlooking the airport

60 One of the tunnels leading to the plane-loading fingers; these were originally to have been equipped with moving pavements

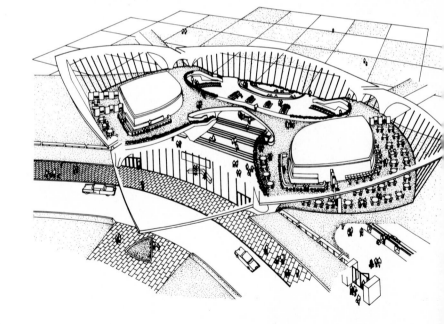

58

61-67, Dulles International Airport (Washington, D.C.), Chantilly, Virginia (1958-62)

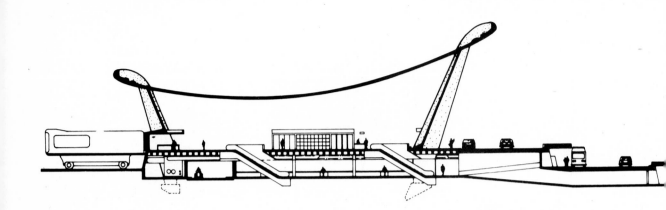

61 Section through terminal building. Both the suspension structure of the main roof and the mobile lounges can be clearly seen

62 Plan of terminal building, showing: 1, main landside entrance; 2, ticket offices; 3, airside customs hall; 4, departure gates for mobile lounges; 5, airside administration buildings and control tower

63 A mobile lounge

64 View towards landside from the principal floor

65 Lateral view of principal floor showing concave glazing, chairs by Charles Eames, and pronounced curvature of suspension roof

66 Side view showing control tower, mobile lounges and heavily glazed suspension structure to main building. Endless lateral expansion was one of Saarinen's aims in conceiving the building as a simple line between land- and airsides

67 Main entrance showing concave glazing designed to defeat the opaque effect of flat glazing as used on the Kresge auditorium at M.I.T. (pl. 15)

62

0   30m

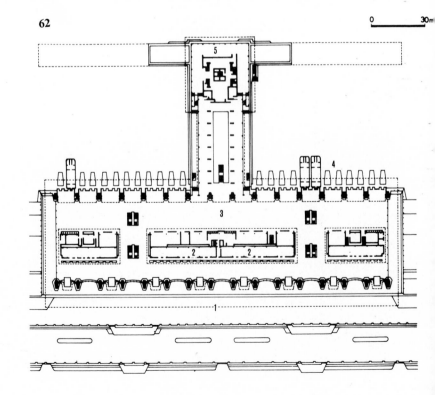

68-72, University of Chicago: Women's Dormitory and Dining Hall, Chicago, Illinois (1955-58)

68 Outside corner of the three-sided dormitory block

69

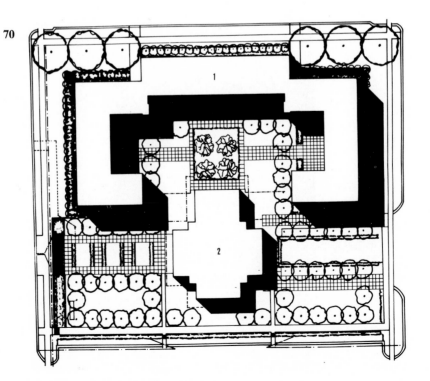

70

69 The dining hall block

70 Site plan of entire complex, showing: 1, dormitories; 2, dining hall

71 Ground-floor entrance lobby to dining hall

72 Ground-floor (left) and first-floor (right) plans of dormitory and dining hall, showing: 1, student bedrooms; 2, lounges at ground-floor level; 3, common room; 4, cafeteria; 5, kitchens

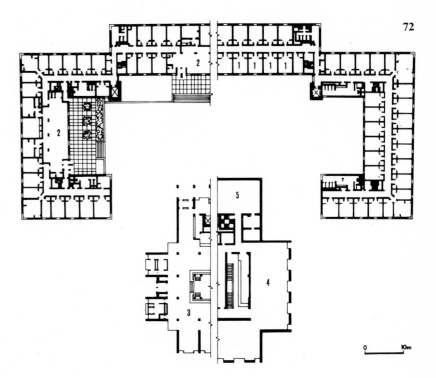

72

73-75, University of Pennsylvania: Women's Dormitories, Philadelphia, Pa (1957-60)

73 External view of the four dormitory blocks linked by a glazed screen. The eaves detail is formed by curved steel handrailing

74 Typical floor plan of dormitory, showing: 1, study bedrooms; 2, lounges; 3, lavatories; 4, kitchenettes

75 The internal court showing use of indoor planting and contrast between internal and external treatment

73

76-79, Ezra Stiles and Morse Colleges, Yale University, New Haven, Connecticut (1958-62)

76 Site plan showing relationship of Stiles and Morse colleges to the existing Graduate School (bottom right). The half circular block (1) contains study bedrooms, whilst the central building (2) contains the dining hall and community facilities

77 Cast concrete with a masonry facing on the dining hall block. High-level windows and screened slits can be seen

78 The lawn enclosed by the dormitory block

79 The principal dining hall, showing diagonal trussed roof structure, metal light fittings and masonry-faced concrete walls

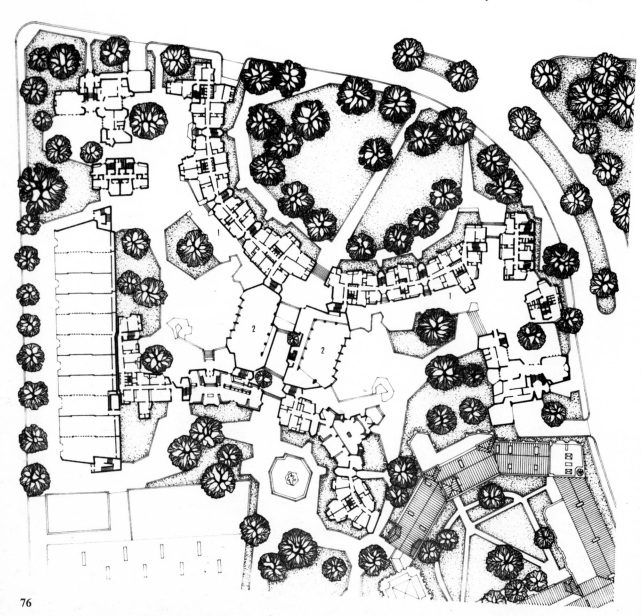

**80-90, Deere & Company headquarters building,
Moline, Illinois (1957-63)**

80

80 Covered way outside
administrative centre, showing
exposed structural steelwork

81, 82 Floor plans showing (left)
exhibition and auditorium areas,
with bridge link, and (right) one
floor of the administrative centre.
Key: 1, exhibition space for
agricultural machinery manufactured
by the company; 2, auditorium;
3, staff dining rooms

83 Side of the administrative
centre, showing flying bridge to
laboratories and steel *brise soleil*

84 The administrative centre seen
from the lake

85 Exterior view of exhibition
building with administrative centre
to the left

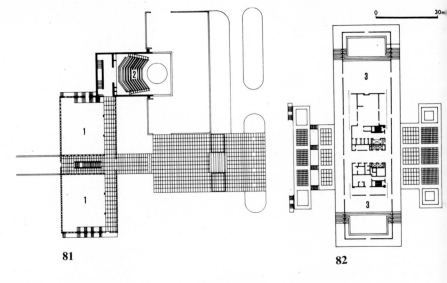

81

82

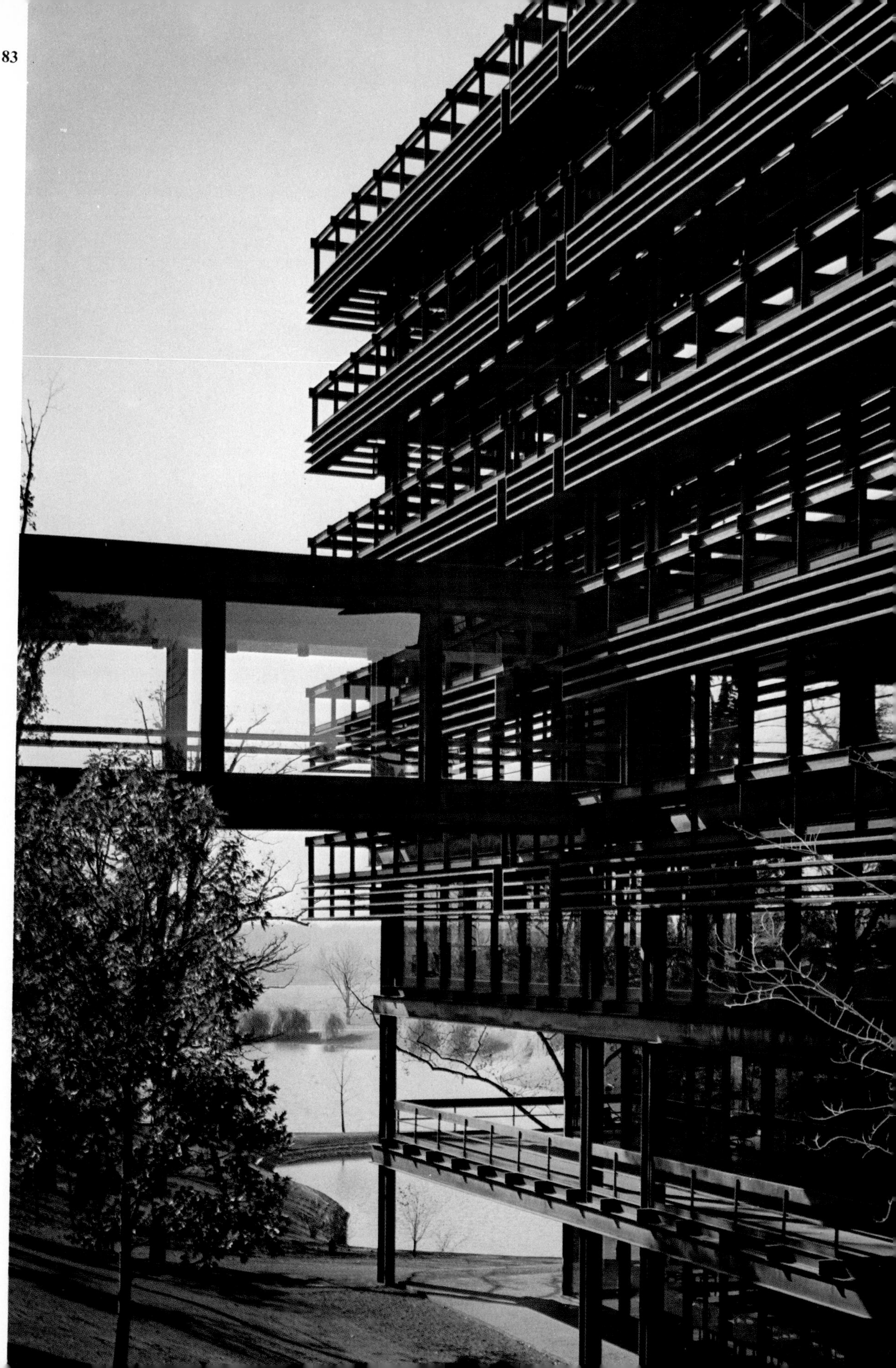

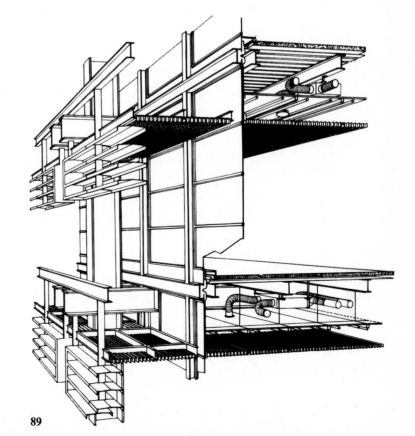

86 Flying bridge from administrative building to exhibition building

87 Exterior of auditorium

88 Section through complex showing administrative building, exhibition building and laboratories

89 Sectional drawing of the administrative building, showing steel details, checkerplate ceilings and arrangement of services between floor and ceiling

90 Interior of exhibition hall

89

91-96, Columbia Broadcasting System headquarters building, New York, N.Y. (1960-64)

91 Section of CBS Building, showing outline of sunken piazza and auxiliary service building

92, 93 Plans of ground floor and typical office floor. Key: 1, main entrance foyers; 2, sub-lettable commercial areas; 3, clear office space on all upper floors

94 The CBS Building (top) with three neighbours. Note the reflection of the lower tower in the tinted windows of the Saarinen tower

95 Main entrance to the CBS Building showing rotating doors inserted between granite-faced concrete columns

96 The CBS Building, showing solid effect of triangular columns viewed obliquely

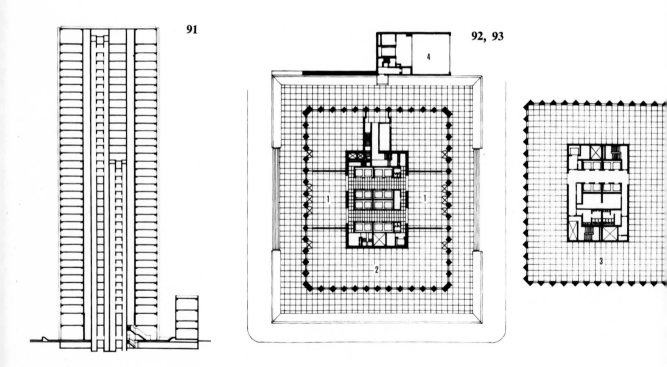

91

92, 93

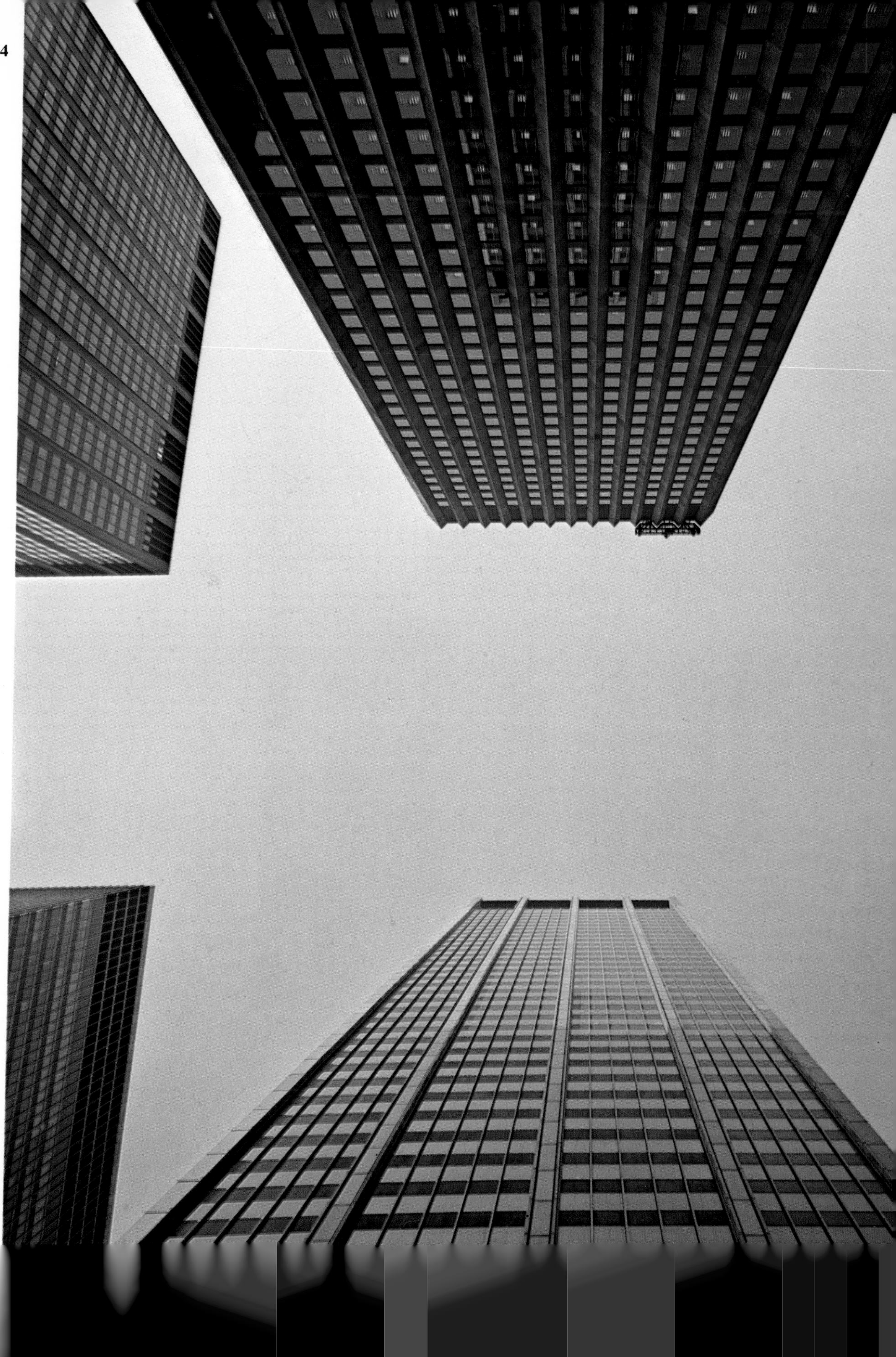

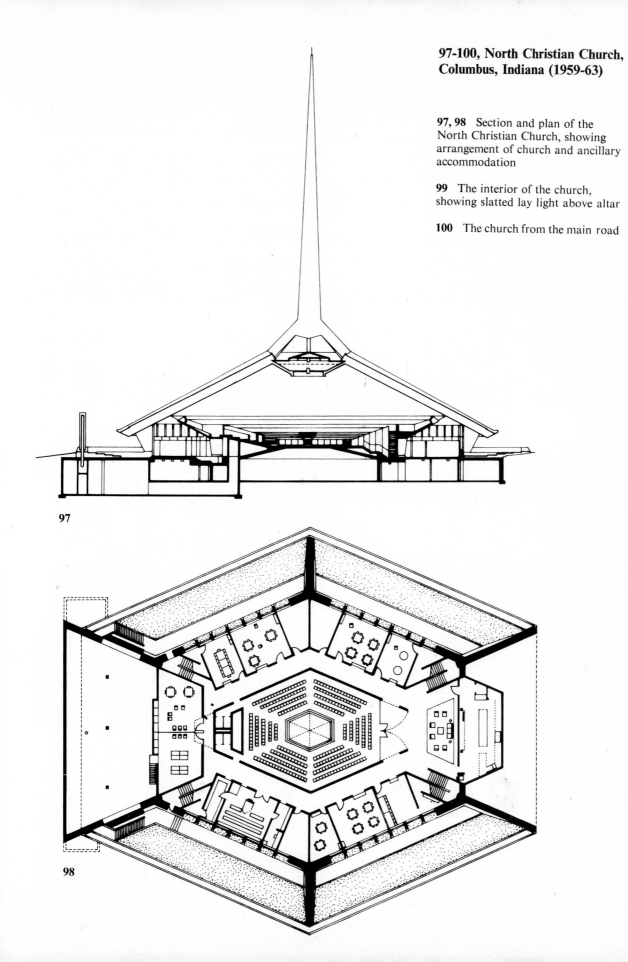

97-100, North Christian Church, Columbus, Indiana (1959-63)

97, 98 Section and plan of the North Christian Church, showing arrangement of church and ancillary accommodation

99 The interior of the church, showing slatted lay light above altar

100 The church from the main road

97

98

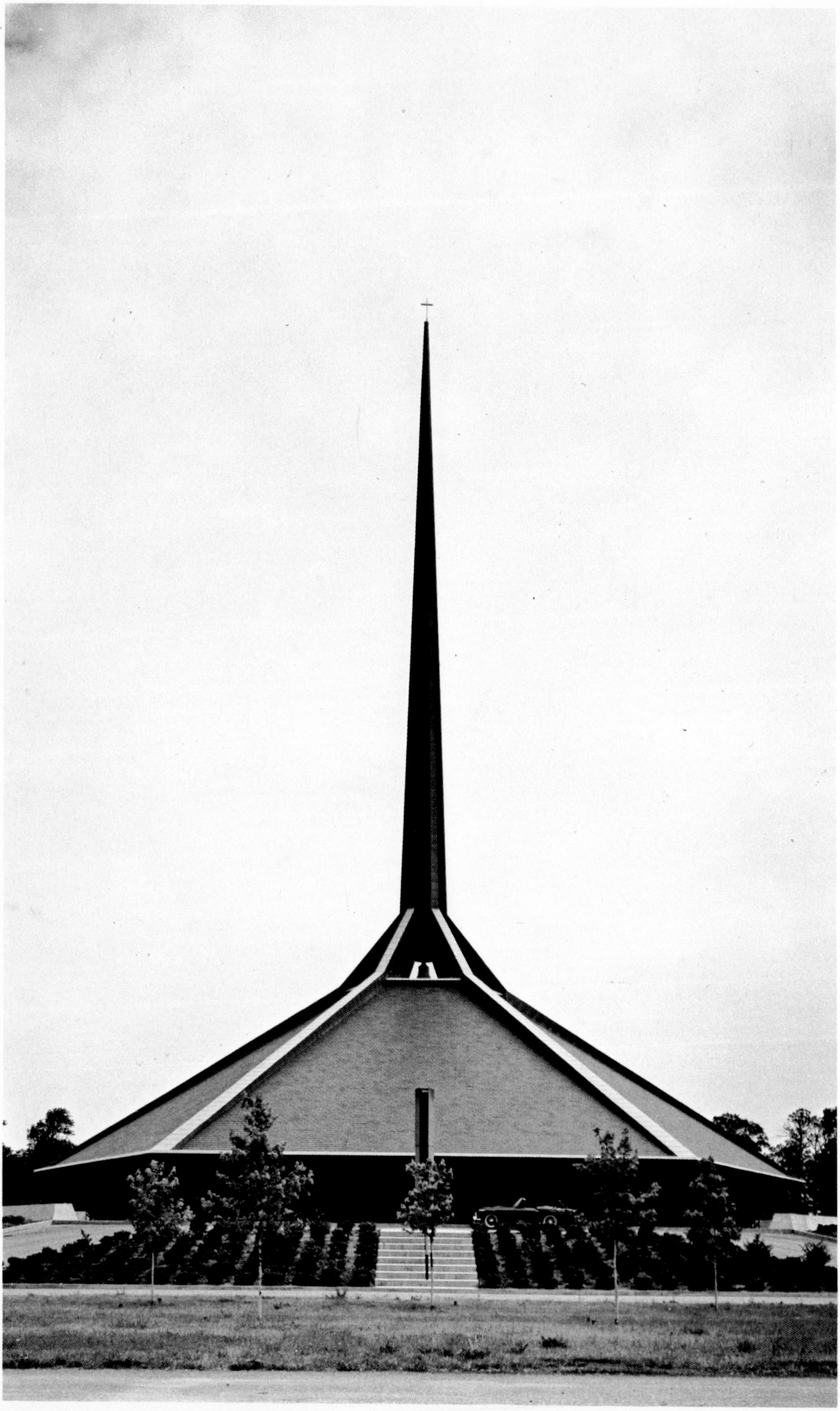

Notes on the plates

/.

1–5
Jefferson Memorial Arch,
St Louis, Missouri
(competition 1947–48;
built 1959–64)

President Jefferson purchased Louisiana in 1803 from Napoleon for fifteen million dollars and in so doing opened the way to the great westward expansion which during the nineteenth century began the conversion of the United States of America from an impoverished former colony into the leading industrial power in the world. The starting point for this great adventure was St Louis on the Mississippi river, and to commemorate the historical event a national competition was held in 1947 for a monument to stand on the banks of the river itself. Both Saarinens, father and son, entered the competition and by an oversight the telegram informing Eero of his victory was addressed to his father. The resultant confusion was quickly resolved but the competition success marked the commencement of Eero's independent career.

His design was for a huge stainless-steel arch, 590 ft high, which—from the opposite bank—would appear as a ring with its reflection in the water. The arch itself was to be a hollow-frame structure incorporating small lift cars to transport visitors to an observation room at the top. During the ten years which intervened between the competition and the execution of the work (a delay resulting from the necessity of removing an old rail terminus) Saarinen altered the design in several important particulars, notably the arrangement of the landscaping at the feet of the tower and the actual profile and height of the arch itself. The finished monument is in fact 40 ft higher than the original competition entry.

6–10
General Motors Technical
Center, Warren, Michigan
(1948–56)

The first major commission which Eero inherited from his father, the General Motors Technical Center grew between 1945 (when it was first proposed in the image of Cranbrook) and 1950 from a 20 million dollar contract to one worth 100 million dollars. Working to a giant scale related to the speed and mobility of the automobile rather than of the human being, Saarinen arranged a number of low, rectangular buildings around an enormous 22-acre lake set in the centre of a 900-acre flat site. The gigantic scale of the arrangement—unlinked by a large planning module such as the 24-metre grid employed by Mies van der Rohe at the Illinois Institute of Technology—tends to present a feeling of brooding, menacing isolation rather than one of technical precision, and this despite the advanced curtain-walling and constructional systems incorporated with the research assistance of the General Motors organization.

11–15
The Kresge Chapel,
Massachusetts Institute
of Technology,
Cambridge, Mass.
(1953–56)

A brick drum 50 ft in diameter, the chapel has seating for only 128 people, and stands in a small pool also of circular form. Low arches set into the base of the wall allow daylight to illuminate the interior by reflection from the pool, whilst the undulating interior skin of brickwork modulates the reflections thus formed so that they do not detract from the artful top-lighting of the altar via a shimmering suspended screen designed by the former Cranbrook teacher, Harry Bertoia. Saarinen derived his inspiration for this building from a recollection of a student visit to Greece when bright moonlight over a mountain village in Sparta had created an effect similar to the one he tried to achieve by the ingenious combination of top and bottom lighting here.

16, 17
The Kresge Auditorium,
Massachusetts Institute
of Technology,
Cambridge, Mass.
(1953–56)

The first large-scale concrete-shell building to be completed in the United States, the Kresge Auditorium is a pure geometric form based on one-eighth part of a sphere cut triangularly so that it rests upon three major supports nearly 150 ft apart. As the sectional view indicates, the raked seating constitutes a second, inverted shell beneath the first. Unfortunately the heavy mass of the dome—which belies a structure fundamentally light—rests so close to the ground that this relationship is theoretical rather than apparent. Similarly the considerable span of the structure is concealed by the opacity of the vertical glazing, which prevents any inward view from a distance (see pl. 15).

18–22
The Law School,
University of Chicago,
Chicago, Illinois (1956–60)

Bearing a strong similarity to the IBM Research Facility at Rochester, Minnesota, the curtain-walling system employed for the Chicago University Law School marks the steady evolution of Saarinen's achievement of an extremely thin, high-performance, transparent curtain between the interior and the exterior of a building. The use of neoprene gaskets (first developed in conjunction with the General Motors Research and Development Group for the Technical Center at Warren, Michigan), reflecting glass (to reduce air-conditioning load), and extremely thin steel support members, combines here to produce a precise, articulated façade of potentially infinite length. The zig-zag outer surface resulted from an effort to relate to the neo-Gothic style of the existing university buildings. In order to emphasize the precision and transparency of the screen wall, a pool was placed in front of the building with free-standing sculptures springing from it. The reflected façade thus achieves the kind of completeness which Saarinen strove for with the reflection of the Jefferson Memorial Arch at St Louis, Missouri.

23–25
U.S. Chancellery building,
London, England
(1955–60)

Built as a result of the architect's success in a closed competition held by the U.S. State Department in 1955, the U.S. Embassy in London was the largest and most expensive of the embassy-building programme carried out during the 1950s. Saarinen's precast-concrete design was intended to retain the Georgian character of Grosvenor Square after its proposed reconstruction in the pseudo-Georgian style by the Grosvenor Estate, to whom the entire square belongs. A result of the architect's attempt to anticipate this redevelopment (as yet uncarried out) has been the breaking up of the enclosing form of the square itself; this stems from a refusal to use the entire width of the site. The front and sides of the building itself were finally clad in Portland stone which Saarinen hoped would blacken gracefully in London's sulphurous atmosphere: unfortunately the effects of anti-pollution legislation have prevented this consummation, and after ten years the bald stone finish, relieved only by gold anodised-aluminium trim, looks as garish as it did upon completion.

26–31
U.S. Chancellery building,
Oslo, Norway (1955–59)

More subdued than its London counterpart, the Oslo Embassy is a triangular building on a triangular site in the centre of the city. It encloses a central court in the manner of a Renaissance *palazzo*, but in deference to the Norwegian climate the court is covered. The façade, articulated in a manner similar to that employed on the London building, is nevertheless given an entirely different aspect by the use of pre-cast-concrete facing elements surfaced in polished Norwegian granite. The result, a finish of a rich dark-green colour, is altogether more impressive than the Portland stone used in London. A cantilevered triangular porch marks the main entrance from the Drammensveien, one of Oslo's principal streets. The triangular form of the building is followed through structurally with the use of a diagonal grid of concrete beams.

32–35
International Business Machines: Thomas A. Watson Research Center, Yorktown, N.Y. (1957–61)

Reversing the orthodoxy of the period, Saarinen designed this IBM research centre with top-lit laboratories and perimeter corridors, the party walls between laboratories serving as servicing zones. This basic arrangement enabled the architect to design the whole complex in the form of a glazed, crescent-shaped façade, 1,000 ft long, around the top of a small hill. Expansion was to be gained by the extension of the crescent into a full circle around a court already landscaped as a Japanese garden. The use of corridors on external walls enabled the architect to achieve a uniform curtain wall along the full length of the façade without sill levels or differential glazing. The resultant nearly opaque façade represents one of his greatest achievements in the field of light screening structures of high performance. Curving against the crescent swing of the main building is a low random-rubble wall with sculptures by Seymour Lipton at each end. The same indigenous walling material is used internally and externally and serves as a foil to the precise glazing details.

36–40
Bell Telephone Corporation Research Laboratories, Holmdel, New Jersey (1957–62)

Intended to house 4,000 scientific workers, the Bell Research Laboratories at Holmdel consist of four rectangular buildings enclosed by a massive curtain-wall system glazed with reflective glass to reduce the air-conditioning load of such an enormous glazed volume. The building itself lies at the centre of an enormous landscaped ellipse, itself penetrated by two smaller ellipses defined by roads and trees and extending across a grass strip about 100 ft wide. Inside the enclosing glass wall the same arrangement of perimeter corridors and back-to-back laboratories sharing service walls is employed as that first installed in the IBM Research Center at Yorktown, N.Y. The superblock itself is composed of two long, rectangular units, each 700 ft long by 135 ft wide.

41–43
Irwin Union Bank and Trust Company, Columbus, Indiana (1952–55)

Columbus, Indiana, possesses four works by Eero Saarinen, including the only house he ever designed, the Miller residence. The Irwin Union Trust Company building is a comparatively early work which appears as a single-storey glazed building. It is in fact the visible portion of a three-part complex comprising a basement containing bank vaults, conference and dining rooms, a separate blank-walled office building, and the glazed banking hall itself. The open banking hall was one of the first to be built in the USA, although the technique of relying on the security of clear vision from without is more common today. The large circular apertures in the roof of the banking hall are in fact reflectors for upward pointing spotlights.

44–47
Milwaukee County War
Memorial, Milwaukee,
Wisconsin (1953–57)

Sited at the top of a rise in comparatively flat country, the Memorial is a reinforced-concrete box structure which cantilevers twenty feet in three directions from a square base. The central square formed by the three overhanging boxes is hollow, structural rigidity being assured by the integral reinforcement of roof and floor slabs via the wall intersections of the hollow and solid squares. As noted in the introduction, the detailing of this building, particularly as regards the staircases and interior finishes, scarcely lives up to the promise of the formal conception. Saarinen himself later noted that an 'organic' quality was missing in the completed building.

48–52
David S. Ingalls Hockey
Rink, Yale University,
New Haven, Connecticut
(1956–59)

Bearing an odd resemblance to an inverted boat, the Ingalls Hockey Rink was originally designed around a huge steel truss (forming as it were the keel of the boat), from which tension cables were to reach to the ground on either side, supporting the roof as they did so. As the design progressed, Saarinen and the consulting engineer, Fred Severud, saw the advantages of using a reinforced-concrete parabolic arch instead, and it was in this material that the building was finally completed. In an effort to avoid the apparent massive downward thrust of the concrete dome used at MIT (pls 15–17), Saarinen carried both ends of the arch up in the form of cantilevers—later to incorporate floodlighting designed by the sculptor Oliver Andrews. The roof itself, on either side of the central arch, is supported on cables slung in catenary curves and anchored laterally into the curving side walls of the arena above the seating. These side walls also slope outward to express their support function. The interior of the roof is lined with close timber boarding, whilst the exterior is surfaced with a black neoprene waterproofing solution. Three external cables run from the top of the concrete arch direct to the ground to guarantee stability under snow loading.

53–60
Trans World Airlines
terminal, Idlewild
(now Kennedy) Airport,
New York, N.Y. (1956–62)

Probably Saarinen's most famous design, the TWA terminal was intended to express the drama and excitement of air travel through a structure which appeared at all times to be in motion, constantly changing and transporting the airline passenger. The basic structure itself consists of four interconnected barrel vaults of slightly different shapes supported on four Y-shaped columns. Together these vaults form a vast concrete shell, 50 ft high and 315 ft long, enclosing the whole passenger area of the terminal. Saarinen and his consultant engineers (Ammann and Whitney) carried the basic form of the vaulting through into the design of all the spaces inside and outside the building, with the result that the terminal became one of the most expressionistic structures to be completed in the twentieth century—closely resembling in theme the architecture of Rudolf Steiner and Erich Mendelsohn, but far exceeding either in both scale and excitement. Many of the advanced features intended to be incorporated into the TWA building were omitted for cost reasons or through later reorganizations of passenger flow. These included screens of hot air to replace walls and windows, and moving pavements to transport passengers.

61–67

Dulles International Airport (Washington, D.C.), Chantilly, Virginia (1958–62)

The first commercial airport ever to be conceived from the point of view of jet aircraft operation, Dulles represents in the minds of most critics Eero Saarinen's greatest achievement as a designer. The two principal elements of the airport are the 150-ft span suspension roof over the centralized airport facilities, and the revolutionary 'mobile lounges' to transport passengers to and from aircraft parked at strategic points on the apron. This method of passenger movement was developed by the architect from the use of buses for the same purpose in certain European airports. Its chief advantage lies in the avoidance of miles of pedestrian corridor leading from the terminal to the aircraft—a condition which could be seen at its worst at Chicago's O'Hare airport. The presentation of this revolutionary idea to the client was carried out by means of a film made by Saarinen's long-time collaborator Charles Eames.

Conceiving the main building as a plane 'hovering between earth and sky', Saarinen developed a suspension structure related to that employed on the Ingalls Hockey Rink. Here he used the same catenary cables to carry the roof (this time concrete), outward-leaning concrete columns (echoing the outward-leaning walls at Ingalls), and the same uninterrupted roofscape from within. The reverse curvature of the roof itself derived from the absence of a central arch, but in other respects the thinking underlying the construction was similar, though on a much larger scale.

68–72

University of Chicago: Womens' Dormitory and Dining Hall, Chicago, Illinois (1955–58)

One of many dormitory buildings designed by Saarinen during his decade of individual practice, the Chicago University group was based on a form of alternate glazing and brick panels devised by Matthew Nowicki, a former associate of Saarinen, who died in 1953. In this case the brick panels are replaced by dressed limestone in order to harmonize with existing buildings. The dormitories themselves enclose three sides of a court whose open side is dominated by the dining hall block constructed identically but not linked to the dormitory wing.

73–75

University of Pennsylvania: Women's Dormitories, Philadelphia, Pa (1957–60)

The massive appearance of this brick building is deceptive because in reality it consists of four L-shaped buildings arranged to surround a central court and enclosed for climatic reasons, as in the case of the U.S. Embassy in Oslo. The external elevations of the building, with alternating horizontal and vertical windows set deep into a brick façade, give a curious impression of damaged solidity, whilst the enclosed court with its steel-trussed roof in no way reflects the appearance of the exterior construction.

76–79

Ezra Stiles and Morse Colleges, Yale University, New Haven, Connecticut (1958–62)

Saarinen's task at Yale was to insert two new colleges into the space between a pseudo-Gothic Gymnasium and a similarly styled Graduate School. At the same time conversations with students had led the architect to the conclusion that accommodation in the new colleges should be highly personalized and individualistic. As a result of these two major constraints he devised a polygonal form of building which was to create intimate enclosed spaces on the ground as well as irregularly shaped accommodation. Rejecting contemporary emphasis on large areas of glass, he stressed the rough masonry walls at the expense of windows which are either set high up or shielded in the manner of observation slits in a fortification. The walls themselves are of concrete with a masonry facing.

80–90
Deere & Company headquarters building, Moline, Illinois (1957–63)

The last of Saarinen's major commissions for the construction of rural headquarters for large American corporations, the Deere building straddles an undulating site heavily laced with trees. The principal building of the complex, the administrative centre, is built across the end of a large lake designed by the architect; on either side of it stand smaller buildings (on the slopes of a shallow valley) which are linked to the administrative centre by glazed bridges. The buildings themselves are constructed in a type of steel alloy which develops a copper-like patina when exposed to the elements and thereafter remains almost corrosion-free. This material is used to provide *brise soleil* as well as constituting the structural frame of the complex. All windows are glazed with gold-tinted mirror glass; this reduces the air-conditioning load within the building by reflecting approximately 70 per cent. of solar heat gain. The combination of mirror glass and skeletal steel structure gives the building a curiously insubstantial aspect from the outside.

91–96
Columbia Broadcasting System headquarters building, New York, N.Y. (1960–64)

Billed by the architect as 'the simplest skyscraper in New York', the CBS Building is a free-standing rectangle, 491 ft high, with strongly emphasized vertical elements reaching from top to bottom in the form of triangular concrete columns faced in dark granite. In the ruthless pursuit of simplicity Saarinen eschewed minor tricks of entasis (whereby the thickness of the building decreases with height) and instead arranged for service trunking in the upper half of the building to pass through the inside covering of columns whose actual size was unnecessarily large in view of the load carried. At ground level the CBS requirement for lettable commercial premises, as well as the architect's refusal to break the column grid for main entrance doors, gives the building an extraordinarily forbidding appearance. The dark opacity of the façade is enhanced by the use of tinted glass.

97–100
North Christian Church, Columbus, Indiana (1959–63)

With the plan-form of a flattened hexagon, the North Christian Church incorporates ancillary accommodation beneath the church itself instead of in a separate building. The body of the church is situated above ground level with seating around a central altar; the resulting access via stairs has, in the mind of the architect, something of the quality of an airlock separating profane from spiritual things. The structure of the church itself is totally dominated by the spire which springs from the low-pitched hexagonal roof and contains an open belfry in its base. This opening also provides top-lighting for the altar beneath.

Chronological list: projects and events

1910 Eero Saarinen born on 20 August at Kirkkonummi, Finland

1922 His father, Eliel Saarinen, wins second prize in *Chicago Tribune* competition

1923 The Saarinen family emigrates to the United States

1925 The family settles at Cranbrook, Michigan

1929–31 Studies sculpture in Paris

1930–34 Attends Yale University School of Architecture and subsequently travels in Europe

1936 Returns to Cranbrook and joins father's practice

1939 Marries Lily Swann

1940 Wins, in collaboration with Charles Eames, two first prizes for furniture design, Museum of Modern Art, New York

1942–45 Service in Office of Strategic Studies, Washington, D.C.

1948 Wins Jefferson Memorial competition, St Louis, Missouri (built 1959–64)

1947–55 Drake University, Des Moines, Iowa: pharmacy building (1947–50) and dormitories and dining hall (1951–55)

1948–56 General Motors Technical Center, Warren, Michigan (including furniture design)

1950 Death of Eliel Saarinen

1952–55 Irwin Union Bank and Trust Company, Columbus, Indiana

1953 First marriage ends in divorce; marries Aline B. Louchheim

1953–56 Massachusetts Institute of Technology, Cambridge, Mass.: Kresge Auditorium and Chapel

1953–57 Milwaukee County War Memorial, Milwaukee, Wisconsin; Stephens College Chapel, Columbia, Missouri; Miller house, Columbus, Indiana

1954 Master plan for University of Michigan, Ann Arbor, Michigan

1954–58 Concordia Senior College, Fort Wayne, Indiana; Vassar College dormitory building, Poughkeepsie, New York

1955–58 University of Chicago, Chicago, Illinois: women's dormitory and dining hall

1955–59 U.S. Chancellery building, Oslo, Norway

1955–60 U.S. Chancellery building, London, England
1956–59 International Business Machines, Rochester, Minnesota
1956–60 University of Chicago, Chicago, Illinois: Law School
1956–62 Trans World Airlines terminal building, Idlewild (Kennedy) Airport, New York
1957–60 University of Pennsylvania, Philadelphia: women's dormitories
1957–61 International Business Machines: Thomas J. Watson Research Center, Yorktown, New York
1957–62 Bell Telephone Corporation: Research Laboratories, Holmdel, New Jersey
1957–63 Deere & Company, Moline, Illinois
1958–62 Ezra Stiles and Morse Colleges, Yale University, New Haven, Connecticut; Dulles International Airport terminal building, Chantilly, Virginia
1958–64 Lincoln Center for the Performing Arts, New York, N.Y.: repertory theatre and library museum (in association with Skidmore, Owings & Merrill; collaborating designer for theatre, J. Mielziner)
1959–63 North Christian Church, Columbus, Indiana
1960–64 Columbia Broadcasting System headquarters building, New York, N.Y.; International Airport, Athens, Greece
1961 Saarinen dies, 1 September, at Ann Arbor, Michigan

Select bibliography

By Eero Saarinen

Eero Saarinen on his Work, ed. Aline B. Saarinen, New Haven, Conn., and London, 1962; a selection of buildings with commentaries by the architect

'Six Broad Currents of Modern Architecture', *Architectural Forum*, July 1953

'Changing Philosophy of Architecture', *Architectural Review*, August 1954

'Function, Structure and Beauty', *Architectural Association Journal*, July–August 1957

'Recent Work of Eero Saarinen', in *Zodiac* 4, 1959; contains references to Jefferson Memorial Arch, David S. Ingalls Hockey Rink, TWA terminal, and IBM building at Rochester, as well as coverage of furniture designs

'Campus Planning: the Unique World of the University', *Architectural Review*, November 1960

On Eero Saarinen

Cantacuzino, Sherban G., *Great Modern Architecture*, New York and London, 1966

Temko, Allan, *Eero Saarinen*, London and New York, 1962

'The Maturing Modern', *Time*, 2 July 1956; a profile of the architect

Carter, Peter, 'Eero Saarinen, 1910–1961', *Architectural Design*, December 1961

Haskell, Douglas, 'Eero Saarinen, 1910–1961', *Architectural Forum*, October 1961

Lessing, Lawrence, 'The Diversity of Eero Saarinen', *Architectural Forum*, July 1960

Louchheim, Aline' B., Now Saarinen the Son', *New York Times Magazine*, 26 April 1953

McQuade, Walter, 'Eero Saarinen, a Complete Architect', *Architectural Forum*, April 1962

Temko, Allan, 'Eero Saarinen: Something between Earth and Sky', an interview with the architect, *Horizon*, July 1960

Index

Numbers in italics refer to the plates

airport buildings, *see* Dulles International Airport; Trans World Airlines terminal
Ammann and Whitney (engineers) 17, 18
Andrews, Oliver 122

Bell Telephone Corporation: Research Laboratories (Holmdel, N.J.) 15, 121, *36–40*
Bertoia, Harry 11, 119
Booth, George C. 10
Burnham, Daniel 11

Center Line, Mich. 11
Chicago, University of: Law School 120, *18–22*; Women's Dormitory and Dining Hall 123, *68–72*
Chicago Tribune 10
Clean Air Act (1956) 17
Columbia Broadcasting System headquarters (New York) 16, 124, *91–96*
Cranbrook, Mich. 10, 11

Deere & Company headquarters (Moline, Ill.) 15, 124, *80–90*
Dulles International Airport (Washington, D.C.) 11, 17, 18, 19, 123, *61–67*

Eames, Charles 11, 123
embassy buildings: London 17, 120, *23–25*; Oslo 120, *26–31*

Fry, Maxwell 9
furniture designs 11

Geddes, Norman Bel 11

General Motors Technical Center (Warren, Mich.) 11, 12, 119, *6–10*

Helsinki: Central railway station 10
'Hvitträsk' (house) 10

International Business Machines (IBM): Rochester, Minn. 14, 120; Thomas A. Watson Research Center, Yorktown, N.Y. 15, 121, *32–35*
Irwin Union Bank and Trust Company (Columbus, Ind.) 121, *41–43*

Jefferson Memorial Arch (St Louis, Mo.) 19, 119, *1–5*

Knoll, Florence 11, 16

Massachusetts Institute of Technology: Kresge Auditorium and Chapel 13, 119, 120, *11–17*
Mendelsohn, Erich 14, 122
Michigan, University of 13
Mies van der Rohe, Ludwig 11, 119
Milwaukee County War Memorial 17, 122, *44–47*
Museum of Modern Art (New York) 11

National Housing Association (U.S.A.) 11
North Christian Church (Columbus, Ind.) 124, *97–100*
Nowicki, Matthew 123

O'Hare Airport (Chicago) 123

Paris exhibition (1900) 10
Pennsylvania, University of: Women's Dormitories 123, *73–75*

Rapson, Ralph 11
Roche, Kevin 14

Saarinen, Eliel 9, 10, 11, 12
Seagram Building (New York) 16
Severud, Fred 17, 122
Steiner, Rudolf 122
Swann, Lily 13

Trans World Airlines terminal, Idlewild

(Kennedy) airport 16, 17, 18, 122, *53–60*

Weese, Harry 11
Willow Run, Mich. 11
Wright, Frank Lloyd 11

Yale University 11; Ingalls Hockey Rink 17, 122, 123, *48–52*; Ezra Stiles and Morse Colleges 123, *76–79*